AF575350

FOODS FROM
MEXICO
GOLRIZ GOLKAR
childsworld.com

Published by The Child's World®
800-599-READ • www.childsworld.com

Photography Credits
Photographs ©: Shutterstock Images, cover (background), cover (flag), 1 (background), 1 (flag), 3 (background), 3 (flag), 4 (flag), 5 (globe), 10–11, 13, 16; Boyko Pictures/Shutterstock Images, 4 (landmarks), back cover; Peter Hermes Furian/Shutterstock Images, 5 (country); iStockphoto, 6–7, 8, 20; Gerardo Ramirez Penaloza/iStockphoto, 15; Vitaliy Halenov/iStockphoto, 19; Ezume Images/iStockphoto, 22

ISBN Information
9781503885271 (Reinforced Library Binding)
9781503885684 (Portable Document Format)
9781503886322 (Online Multi-user eBook)
9781503886964 (Electronic Publication)

LCCN 2023937423

Printed in the United States of America

Golriz Golkar is a former elementary school teacher. She has written more than 70 books for children. She enjoys reading, looking for ladybugs, and baking with her young daughter.

TABLE OF CONTENTS

MEXICO

Mexico is a country in the southern part of North America. The United States lies to the north. The Gulf of Mexico and the Caribbean Sea border the east of Mexico. Guatemala and Belize share the southeast border. The Pacific Ocean runs along Mexico to the west and the south. Northern Mexico has hot summers and cold winters. The southern half is mostly warm year-round.

Corn, beans, squash, and rice are used in many Mexican dishes. Flatbreads called *tortillas* are popular. Meat dishes are favorites in the northern and inland areas. Coastal areas enjoy more fish. Desserts and sweet drinks are popular in Mexico. Many Mexicans take lunch breaks with their families. Sometimes, they take an afternoon nap afterward called a *siesta.*

CHAPTER 1

ENCHILADAS

Enchiladas are a popular Mexican food. They were first invented by the Maya **civilization**. The Maya lived in an area called Mesoamerica. It covered parts of modern-day Mexico, Belize, and Guatemala. Around 6,000 years ago, the Maya started growing corn. They pounded it out to make tortillas. They wrapped the tortillas around small fish. These were the first enchiladas.

People have been making corn tortillas for thousands of years.

TEX-MEX ENCHILADAS

In Texas, enchiladas are prepared "Tex-Mex" style. The enchilada sauce is made by mixing chili sauce with brown gravy. Cheddar cheese usually tops the enchiladas instead of Mexican cheese.

Chicken enchiladas can be served with many sides and toppings.

Today, enchiladas are made with many fillings. In Mexico, they are popular for breakfast or lunch. Beef, chicken, fish, or pork are fried in a pan. Beans, onions, corn, and chilies are often added. Red chilies are used to make *rojo* sauce. Green chilies make *verde* sauce. One of these sauces is mixed in with the filling. Sometimes *crema*, or Mexican sour cream, is added.

The filling is placed inside flat corn tortillas. The tortillas are rolled up. They are placed in a baking dish and then covered with toppings. These toppings may include more chili sauce and crema.

The enchiladas are baked in an oven until crispy. After baking, more toppings are added. They include spicy *pico de gallo* salsa and chopped jalapeño or serrano chilies. Cheeses such as tangy *queso blanco* and sweet *cotija* are added. Sliced onion, radishes, and lime wedges are also common toppings. The dish is bursting with many flavors. The texture of the crunchy tortillas pairs with the creaminess of the hot filling. The enchiladas are served with rice and beans.

Pico de gallo salsa is a common topping for enchiladas.

TAMALES

Tamales are another Mexican favorite. They were also invented in Mesoamerica thousands of years ago. The Maya and Aztec peoples enjoyed this dish. It was a simple food that could be eaten on the go. The **ancient** version was made with roasted squash or beans. In the 1500s, Europeans arrived in North America. They brought new foods such as olives, raisins, pork, and chicken. Over time, these foods began to be included in tamale recipes.

A tamale is cooked inside of a corn husk (pictured) or a banana leaf.

Today, tamales are common in Latin America. Tamales are also popular in the Philippines and the Caribbean.

Tamales have many ingredients. Cornmeal flour is mixed with **broth**, cooking fat, and spices. This mixture becomes a soft dough called *masa*. The dough is rolled out. Different fillings are placed in the middle. Fillings usually include cooked and shredded chicken or pork. Carrots, corn, potatoes, and peppers are added. Dried fruits, olives, and cheese are also popular. A smoky, spicy Mexican sauce called *mole* (MOH-lay) is added, too. It is often made with chilies, spices, nuts, and chocolate.

Shredded meat, such as chicken, is usually added to the tamale filling.

MAKING MOLE

Making mole is hard work. Some recipes take up to three days to cook. There are recipes that have as many as 50 ingredients! When the sauce is ready, it is served on special occasions such as weddings, holidays, and other family events.

Tamales are traditionally shaped by hand.

The dough is then closed up. It is cut into brick-shaped pieces. The pieces are wrapped in dried corn husks or banana leaves. The tamales are steamed. The masa hardens, and the filling heats up. When the tamales are finished steaming, the wrappers are removed. Only the dough and filling are eaten. The soft, hot masa dough and spiciness from the filling gives the tamales a **savory** flavor.

Tamales are a common everyday meal. They are also eaten on special holidays such as *Día de la Candelaria*. This Christian holiday is also known as Candlemas. After going to church, families and friends enjoy a tamale feast together.

CHURROS

One favorite Mexican dessert is the *churro.* It was invented in Spain. Spanish explorers brought the recipe to the Americas. Churros arrived in Mexico in the 1800s.

In Mexico, churro shops called *churrerías* sell this sweet, fried treat. Street **vendors** sell them, too. They are also popular in the United States and other countries. Churros are often sold at theme parks in the United States.

Churros are deep-fried and then covered in sugar.

Churros are long strips of fried dough. Flour, butter, and vanilla are mixed to make the dough. Sometimes eggs are added. Once the dough is ready, it is placed inside a **pastry** bag with a star-shaped tip. The tip gives the churros a ridge pattern. The dough is piped into long strips on a tray.

Customers can buy churros from street vendors. The sweet, warm treat can be enjoyed on the go.

The dough strips are then placed in hot cooking oil. Sometimes the dough is piped right into the oil. The churros fry until they become golden. When they are done frying, they are placed on paper towels. This helps remove the extra oil. Then they are rolled in sugar. Churros are sometimes rolled in cinnamon, too. Many Mexicans also dip them in chocolate sauce. These sweet and chewy fritters melt in the mouth!

WONDER MORE

Wondering about New Information

How much did you know about Mexican food before reading this book? What new information did you learn? Write down two interesting facts that this book taught you. Was the information surprising? Why or why not?

Wondering How It Matters

Why do you think it is important to learn about foods from different countries? How can learning about and trying new foods affect your life? Are there any foods from Mexico you would like to try?

Wondering Why

Some Mexican foods such as mole are prepared for special occasions. Why do you think certain foods are eaten on holidays and at important events?

Ways to Keep Wondering

Mexican food is popular in the United States, but recipes can be very different. After reading this book, what questions do you have about Mexican food? What can you do to learn more about how Mexican food is made differently in the United States?

CHICKEN ENCHILADAS RECIPE

After mastering this recipe with an adult's help, try adding other toppings such as sliced jalapeños, pico de gallo, or cotija cheese!

Ingredients

- 1 ½ cups precooked shredded chicken
- 2 cups canned red or green enchilada sauce, divided
- 8 corn tortillas
- 2 ½ cups shredded Mexican-blend cheese
- Salt and pepper for seasoning
- Sour cream and lime wedges (optional)

Steps

1. Preheat oven to 350°F.
2. In a large bowl, combine the cooked shredded chicken with ¼ cup enchilada sauce. Season with salt and pepper.
3. Wrap the tortillas in a moist paper towel and warm them in a microwave for 1 minute.
4. Fill each tortilla with the chicken mixture and sprinkle shredded cheese on top. Roll tightly and lay them seam downward in a large baking dish.
5. Pour the rest of the enchilada sauce over the tortillas and top with more cheese.
6. Bake for 20 minutes, until cheese is gooey. Serve with sour cream and lime wedges, if desired.

GLOSSARY

ancient (AYN-shint) When something is ancient, it means that it existed a long time ago. Enchiladas and tamales were both invented in ancient times.

broth (BRAHTH) A broth is a clear soup made from vegetables or meat. Broth adds liquid and flavor to a dish.

civilization (sih-vil-uh-ZAY-shun) A civilization is a large group of people who share advanced ways of living. The Aztec civilization once made tamales.

pastry (PAY-stree) A pastry is a sweet baked good made from dough. A churro is a type of sweet and fried pastry.

savory (SAY-vuh-ree) When a food is savory, it tastes salty or spicy. Many kinds of spices make a tamale taste savory.

vendors (VEN-durz) Vendors are people who sell things. Street vendors in Mexico often sell churros.

FIND OUT MORE

In the Library

Doeden, Matt. *Travel to Mexico.* Minneapolis, MN: Lerner, 2022.

Kelly, Tracey. *The Culture and Recipes of Mexico.* New York, NY: Rosen, 2017.

Rudolph, Jessica. *Mexico.* Minneapolis, MN: Bearport, 2016.

On the Web

Visit our website for links about foods from Mexico:
childsworld.com/links

Note to Parents, Caregivers, Teachers, and Librarians: We routinely verify our Web links to make sure they are safe and active sites. So encourage your readers to check them out!

INDEX